Next
OF
KIN

*How to Pick a
Compatible Mate.*

Hishiar
Shamdin

authorHOUSE®

AuthorHouse™
1663 Liberty Drive
Bloomington, IN 47403
www.authorhouse.com
Phone: 1 (800) 839-8640

Published by AuthorHouse 04/14/2020

ISBN: 978-1-7283-5777-5 (sc)
ISBN: 978-1-7283-5775-1 (hc)
ISBN: 978-1-7283-5776-8 (e)

Library of Congress Control Number: 2020905888

Dedication

This book is dedicated to my brother, Qidar,
who was always there for me.

Contents

What makes the Husband and Wife the next of Kin to each other?

This relation is legal and true to the law. After you read this book, it would be obvious to you why it is true to law, that the wife or husband, in a compatible marriage are the closest Next of Kin to each other.

Therefore, the more compatible you get, the closet to law you get.

The more incompatible you get, the more legalizing arguments you would need to justify being nest of kin to each other.

We should be happier the more true and legal we get, shouldn't we?

What are The Things that are Important to You in A Woman?

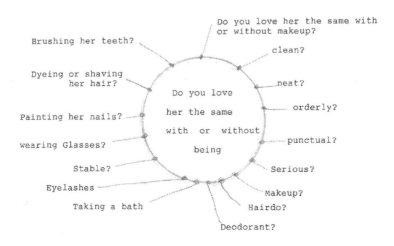

Illustration 1a)

Does She Feel the Same Way About You?

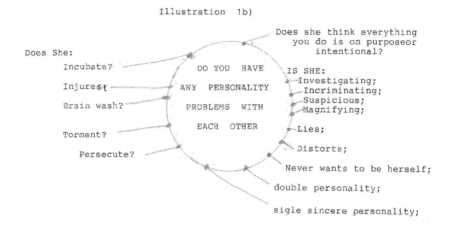

Illustration 1b)

Does She:

Incubate?

Injures?

Brain wash?

Torment?

Persecute?

DO YOU HAVE
ANY PERSONALITY
PROBLEMS WITH
EACH OTHER

Does she think everything
you do is on purposeor
intentional?

IS SHE:
Investigating;
Incriminating;
Suspicious;
Magnifying;
Lies;
Distorts;
Never wants to be herself;
double personality;
sigle sincere personality;

Behavior–

A stable behavior is always the same and predictable. It is nice but not always in the best advantage of the man or woman,

When you are in, not for true love but to irritate, then you act phony; test reaction ; act inconsistently in phony games.

The result is a situation which is worst that when you started.

It is a problem when you think of a woman that she is more decent than she really is. That is where mistakes are made.

A Compatible Woman Would Love You The Way You are Even if You:

Just sit; do nothing; lazy; have no solution; do not care; don't go out; have no initiative.

Of course no man is always like that, but an incompatible woman likes to nag and always accuse you of this and that. Nagginess is an incentive-killing behavior.

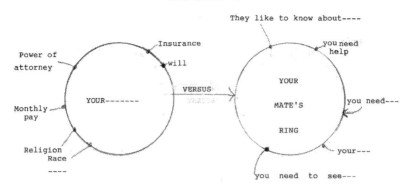

Illustration 2

Personality Traits:

What are the personality traits? How would you know what your personality traits are? How are they graded? How are they instilled (?) to share with the mate of the opposite sex, who have similar compatibility personality traits?

The number of personality traits used to match you with those of the opposite sex depends on where you are going to be matched. Some use seven traits, others use 10 traits. Still others may use different numbers.

<u>Seven Traits</u>	<u>10 Traits</u>
Values	Sociability
Patience	Conformity
Religion	Tranquility
Sex	Dependability
Standards & Ideals	Stability
Sociability	Standards & Ideals
Character	Standing
	Flexibility
	Serious ness
	Family

Your answers to questionnaire, which determines your personality traits, and you are graded on each trait from 0 to 10 or 11. When you are matched through a computer, with mates and the computer sites those mates most compatible with you.

For example, if you are matched using the seven traits, you are considered infatuated, not in love, or truly compatible, if you match on three of the seven personality traits. You should actually match on all seven traits, within 3 grades, except perhaps one trait before you are considered 100% compatible for marriage.

After you are matched by the computer- which is a blind date- you do have a date based on solid grounds. Then comes the meeting—judgement by sight, which either increases or decreases the compatibility. But remember that the final decision is yours. These tests and the computer help you to be exposed to a greater number of mates, therefore, and increases your compatibility chances, and improves it. It is based on sound principles and is good.

Who is the most favorable next of kin?
Favorable signs in Man-woman compatibility:

Mental attraction or love.
Physical attraction or love

She is favorable according to your judgement. You have no will power problem with her. The desire to will in each others name with no reaction or mental reservation, with no cultural or religious difficulties that you have to labor to overcome with no success. There is meeting of the minds of the two of you, lack of use of foul language between the two of you. No jealousy problems, only trust. No wandering of the mind, like wanting to be with the other woman, or wandering about them, and she with a wondering mind about other men and wanting to be with them.

No experience of having any other sexual relations with others: This might initiate meandering of your minds during intercourse and results in your psycho blockage, resulting in temporary impotence. Double personality is not favorable. Your love is so that you don't have to put up with each other. When not ashamed of each other's environment, and having similar drinking and smoking habits, leads to understanding each other's feelings in life, whether it be professional of personal.

SIMILAR PERSONALITY TRAITS:

No difference in outlook about children by previous marriages;
Your likes or dislikes to having pets are similar;
Similar buying taste.
No age problems, even if different.
No irritation as to previous escorts.
You know about each other's previous sexual activities and still love.
Frank about your previous activity; drugs; alcohol; smoking; sexual behavior—normal and abnormal, etc.
No underground marriage or escort ring activities.
Hiding things, especially those that are sensitive, will certainly create ill will and trouble.
When you do not intentionally trouble each other.
When love is genuine and not for the purpose of paying debts, supporting children by previous marriages or ex-husbands, or previous escorts.
Housing with ethics.
Not being promiscuous or adulterous.
Having good taste.
Sexual sincerity that lacks aggravation and prevents you from adultery, masturbation and perversion.

Social sincerity when dating prior to engagement and marriage.

Respect for each other's sensitivity when you think of each other as equal.

No ring activities.

No Nagginess. Nagging is the source of great evils.

Enjoying being together regardless of time and after sexual activities.

Enjoying each other sexually in a harmonious way—without offending each other and with an attitude that makes both of you look forward to the next time, with love and affection.

When you both have the qualities of improving your each other's psychosexual importamce.

No fertility problems that might endanger your relations.

No I.Q. or mental capacity problems.

When you have the feeling and understanding of having a husband and she understands and knows what a wife means.

When you both have an all around feeling that you are each other's Next of Kin.

Not influenced by others.

No superficial wishy washy attitudes.

When you don't involve others in your affairs needlessly and to your disadvantage.

When you both discourage others from discussing you sexually, mentally or professionally.

Professional Compatibility:

When your presence together makes you more sexy; more humorous; happy; content; cheerful and clear.

Abundance of warmth, sincerity, integrity, perseverance and mutual understanding.

The feeling that you could make a successful husband and wife.

You have the tendency to have the same judgement and will power on things and you make close decisions.

When you both have the same opinion as to how you should get married and by whom.

When you both have a manageable personality. If one of you has a bachelor personality, then companionship is better until things change.

When you both have the same understanding, confidence and independence and the same ideas as to what constitutes invasion of privacy.

People having different personality traits than both of you are probably poor as far as understanding you.

Compatible couples of similar personality traits make better companions socially.

Avoid those who are not capable of solving your problems to your thinking.

Forceful quackery to smear you and get ahead of you in the name of solving your problems is no good. The net result is stalling and difficulty in all aspects of your life.

It takes sometimes a great deal of intelligence, sometimes initiative, legal maneuvers, tolerance and suffrage to free yourself from their injustice—a great problem to society.

Who is an Average American—

The average American is honest, sincere, private, minds his/her own business and not in for money alone. His/her love is true and genuine and not for money only. It is for what the other person is.

The average American is simple and open, not suspicious or secretive. They enjoy independence, freedom, love and happiness. They are also clean, neat, orderly and have a good taste. Added to that are the qualities of being artistic, musical, intelligent, considerate, affectionate and enjoys good company. They will care for their health and the health of others. They travel to upgrade their basic requirements for life, liberty and happiness. They enjoy the beauty of nature and are scientific minded and like to improve and be more honest and try not to hold a grudge. The average American does not claim false bravery or brag about it. He/she does not engage in unproductive or useless activities voluntarily or foolishly. They are brave and dependable in times of crisis in the line of duty. They are also sensitive, moral and private. Furthermore, they care about the pride, integrity and self-respect of others.

Chapter

4

Stick to Your Compatibility:

It is best that we stick to our basics in compatibility and personality traits and enjoy it with a similar mate. It is only by treating yourself sincerely and nicely that you become capable of being nicer to others, and thus spread joy and happiness.

You have to practice what you think is right. Marriage to an incompatible mate is the surest way to personality clashes and unhappiness. For a man, it is better to stay a bachelor than to marry an incompatible woman, at least when you have failed in your marriage the first time.

The consequences of sexual relations with an incompatible woman, although better than masturbation, a sexual act, might get you into trouble, and blind you from finding a compatible wife. Avoid incompatibility and its "red tape", and persecutions and take the path of compatibility; it is more enjoyable.

Signs of Compatibility for the man:

Love.

Attraction.

Harmony of love, will power and judgement .

Lack of malice in what she does.

Feeling of compatibility when you are at parties, dinners, meetings or associations with other people.

Lack of irritations.

Lack of telling each other what to do,

Lack of building each others tolerance or testing each others reactions in the wrong direction or beyond each others capacity,

Lack of putting up with each other.

Lack of problems that destroy your sexual life in favor of other things.

Lack of conflict between professional life and sexual life.

Lack of always getting after each other to do things.

Lack of quack interference, stepping on your freedom for no good reason and channeling you to an unhappy situation through psychiatric and religious quackery.

Lack of a personality that entices and encourages mental prostitution or encourages others to abuse your human right.

When both of you are judged by other people as compatible without considering mental recipe factors or red tape.

The woman having a personality that does not entice people to a mentality of putting her man on a tract vulnerable to incriminations and injuries.

When you both warm to each other more than the wills or Insurance you are going to collect.

Lack of a superficial wishy washy oscillation from day to day.

The ability to satisfy each other sexually when you are in the mood.

What Makes Social Life Unhappy in a Community?

To whom? To all? To few? To one?

When we see a compatible couple (How do we know they are compatible? We query), it looks good; it creates happiness and you wish the same for yourself.

When you see and incompatible couple you do not wish the same for yourself. Your compatible wife is an asset to your profession. She does not come second to your profession, nor first since there is no conflict; she is not competing with your profession. She is not a bother, because she is not in to be famous through you. When the only thing she loves about you is to make you famous with no regards to you as a human being, then you are in trouble. The best way to be famous is to be yourself and not to labor to get there. A great many people become famous because they did not mean to be so. To be looking for fame at the expense of your health, sex, love, eating habits, hobbies etc., is not the best way to get there.

What Makes A Woman (Wife) The Right Social Companion?

She invites only couples that her husband and she enjoy their company. She always consults her husband prior to inviting anybody.

She never invites anybody that could be the source of secret activity and mental prostitution.

She never invites previous escorts and social companions. Actually women in this category also must have a history of previous misconduct and have avoided sources of marital troubles, because they thought of these things ahead and behaved in a way that paved the way to a happy marital future. She cares for her husband's profession and cares and helps him to preserve his relations to his good associates and friends.

She is sincere and honest, has good ethics and she looks right for him socially.

She loves her husband the way he is and is never pushy.

She does not engage in mentally disturbing her husband professionally and financially.

She helps her husband and does not take sides with other people against him.

She is interested in professional ethics and does not create inter professional troubles.

She enjoys vacationing with her husband and refuses to counsel him prior to doing things.

She enjoys and knows how to please herself and him after work, on weekends and on vacations.

She enjoys going out with him anywhere. She never tries to pick on her husband and turn him to a "maid habituation" whenever he is home.

She is never frigid and enjoys sexual life to the maximum with him.

Her mind never wanders about other men because she found him the sincere compatible way.

Some Points in Compatibility—

If you do not belong or like to belong to secret societies it would be impossible for you to have a compatible happy marriage, if your mate is engaged in secret society operations of the injurious kind.

In such a setup everything is more important than you. You are simply needed not as a marriage partner but a "second class in a mental recipe" body.

This is kind of nice for the other partner because your marriage legalizes your walking backward and losing everything you have within the law.

Then you get your "within the law" marriage dissolution.

This gives you an "in & out second-class status" in that particular marriage that you foolishly consented to.

That is the way things are in a mental recipe.

Illustration 3

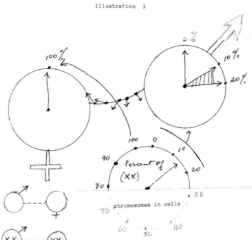

chromosomes in cells

Females- have predominance of (XX)chromosomes
Males- have predominance of (XY)chromosomes.
   Perhaps not more as % of the cell population
   have visible female (xx)chromosomes in the
   nucleus of lineal smears.
In the small circles- (XX) indicate predominance
   of female sex chromosomes and (XY) predominance
   male sex chromosomes.

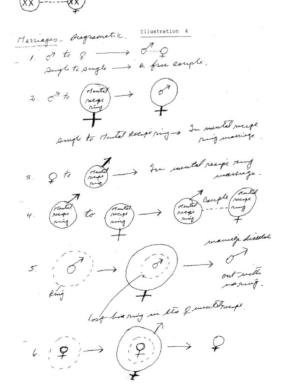

Marriages- Diagramatic.   Illustration 4

1. ♂ to ♀ ⟶ ♂...♀
    Single to single ⟶ a free couple.

2. ♂ to (Mental recipe ring) ⟶ ♂ / ♀
    Single to Mental Recipe ring ⟶ In mental recipe
                                    ring marriage.

3. ♀ to (Mental recipe ring) ⟶ Free mental recipe ring
                                    marriage.

4. (Mental recipe ring) to (Mental recipe ring) ⟶ (Mental recipe ring) Couple (Mental recipe ring) / ♀

5. (Ring ♂) ⟶ (♂ / ♀) ⟶ ♂ marriage dissolved
                                out with
                                no ring.
    lost his ring in the ♀ mental recipe.

6. (♀) ⟶ (♀ / ♀) ⟶ ♀

Illustration 5

Marriage - Diagramatic

THESE LOOK COMPATIBLE.

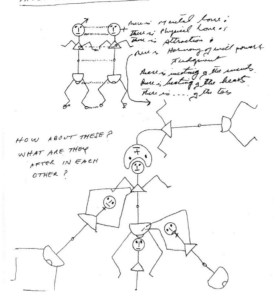

HOW ABOUT THESE?
WHAT ARE THEY
  AFTER IN EACH
  OTHER ?

Chapter

6

The Most Compatible:

Man should seek a most compatible woman. That way you do not stuff your brain (computer) with all the useless things in life for yourself. You eliminate all the incompatibility unhappy time and convert it into happy productive time.

That way you have your brain and hers polished instead of letting it rust and fall apart.

By polishing her brain, she becomes more beautiful and sexy and a better companion, fiancée or wife. When you and your wife are truly compatible, then things work out spontaneously and in the best interest of both of you.

If you happen to be a doctor you will have no practice difficulties and would not need to see anybody for your troubles because you will have none left.

The Most Incompatible:

Those with mental recipe problem usually eat into your pockets; your mental and physical fitness and into your liberty and pursuit of happiness.

They make everything difficult for you and operate rings around you even at times after your marriage is dissolved. They are expert in legalizing illegalities.

With mental recipes, domestic or foreign, first or second class operations, they do insult some of our people in societies and abuse their constitutional rights beyond their capacities. They could be dangerous to health, happiness and liberty.

Why do we have to be sick, unhappy, not free and always mouthed if we are not of the same mental recipe? We should not: why do we have to move over for them to take advantage of us? Well, there is a problem there.

Chapter

7

∽

What Do Men and Women Think About Each Other? How Do You Become The Most Compatible?

The first impression about a woman is important.

To put up with what makes you unhappy with what you see in a woman is not a good idea. That could lead you to personality disorders and will eat into your conscience. It is better to be bold from the start than to put up with years of unhappiness which is not fair for both of you. One should be practical and consider the time factor.

Suppose you think she is frigid. She is frigid because you do not appeal to each other to the maximum. If you do not like her hair or teeth or there is something in her features you do not like; if her skin is not sexy looking enough for you; her legs might add to your frigidity factors. Her body as a whole might not be sexy enough to your senses which would lead you to a frigid outlook.

When there is frigidity based on lack of sexual appeal for each other's body, then your sexual intimacy and sexual activity becomes less satisfying. A sexually incompatible woman is not always a substitute to masturbation. It is not that you keep looking for a compatible partner. There is no true sexual satisfaction outside of being with a compatible woman. Anything else is never as good as is mostly abnormal.

When you both are able to know each other in a crowd then it is a good sign in compatibility.

If you make each other jealous is a bad sign. It means you have failed to understand each other regardless of the reason and that usually eats into every aspect of your life and makes you sexually frigid and unhappy.

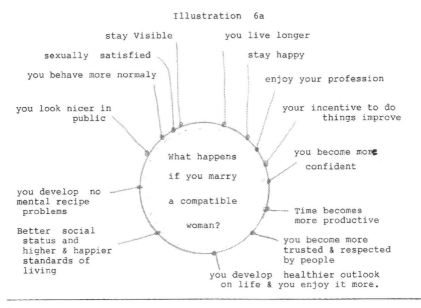

Illustration 6a

stay Visible — you live longer
sexually satisfied — stay happy
you behave more normaly — enjoy your profession
you look nicer in public — your incentive to do things improve

What happens if you marry a compatible woman?

you become more confident
you develop no mental recipe problems
Time becomes more productive
Better social status and higher & happier standards of living
you become more trusted & respected by people
you develop healthier outlook on life & you enjoy it more.

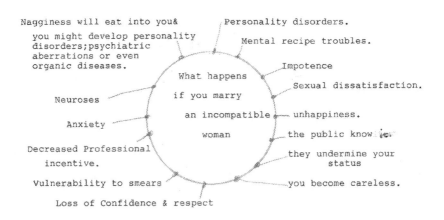

Illustration 6b

Nagginess will eat into you& — Personality disorders.
you might develop personality disorders;psychiatric aberrations or even organic diseases. — Mental recipe troubles.
Impotence
Sexual dissatisfaction.

What happens if you marry an incompatible woman

Neuroses — unhappiness.
Anxiety — the public know
Decreased Professional incentive. — they undermine your status
Vulnerability to smears — you become careless.
Loss of Confidence & respect

Vital Points in Compatibility Between A Man & A Woman:

Age; personality traits; attraction; Mental love; physical love; sex; voice; buying taste; will power; honesty; truthfulness; I.Q.; mental capacity; humor; Heart; mind; acumen; Impulse; common sense.

When compatible you naturally and without mental reservation like to buy things for each other and write wills in each other's name. When things get one-sided only then it is a sign of incompatibility.

Do you naturally believe she is your equal or do you feel deceived?

Is she frigid, irritating and frustrating? Does she make you less sexy and less humorous?

Are your manners and eating habits less natural than when you are with her?

Is she polite, nice and tolerant only when she has her own way? Instead of your way?

Is it usually best to avoid the following: Nagginess; frigidity; malice; race and religious quackery; infatuation; impersonating; swearing and deceiving personalities.

Being less sexy and less humorous than you, are signs of incompatibility. Your feelings when you are with your female are important.

Do you feel happy; content; secure; sincere; independent; equal, respecting, would behave peaceful and just? Are you pleasing naturally? Is your love for your profession altered?

If you get involved in a compatibility problem, you become a responsible person wasting the best and most honest relations with a woman. Such a status of thinking puts on your way to finding one.

Compatibility involves a large number of points among which are: Her age; Looks; Health; Education; economic status; maturity; cleanliness; neatness; orderliness; hobbies; pets; children; relatives; incentive; her feelings about others; benevolence; does she have children by previous marriages?; are her parents coaching?

The nature of her hobbies—swimming; cycling; exercise; music; dancers; dancing; fishing; sailing; skiing; photography; week-end trips; dining out; going to movies; in town compatible socials; in house pleasurable relaxing time and leisure inducing professional incentive and love of life; gardening; cooking; reading; listening to the radio; watching television; Tennis; Pin Pong; Chess; billiard; Hiking; flying; Racing; Painting and writing.

9

Checking into Marriage or Dissolution:

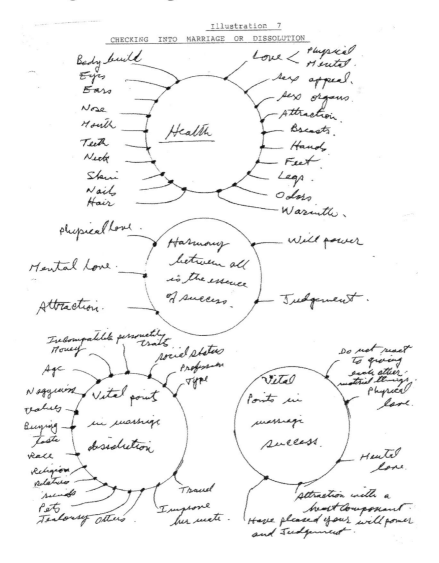

Illustration 7

CHECKING INTO MARRIAGE OR DISSOLUTION

WHAT ARE YOU ENTITLED TO KNOW ABOUT EACH OTHER?
Illustration 8a

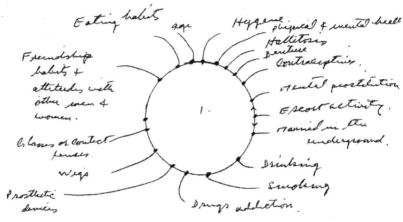

Illustration 8b

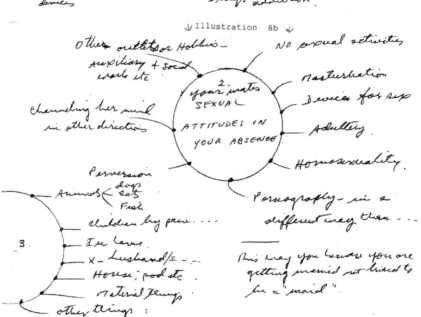

Chapter

10

What are Your Mate's Health Qualifications for Marriage?

IS THERE A HISTORY OF :

Congenital disease—for example Hemophilia; chromosome linked diseases, somatic or sex-linked; dominant or recessive.

Mental illness.

Criminal tendencies; Jail records; Malice.

Cancer.

Arteriosclerosis.

Diabetes.

Alcoholism; smoking; drug habits.

Obesity.

Headaches.

Longevity in the family.

Body odors.

Sterility; Impotence; Frigidity.

Personality—Content; Naggy; trouble maker;

Bachelor type or marriageable;

Humble or arrogant; suspicious;

Paranoid; self-centered.

Occupation and social status;

Religious outlook—orthodox or liberal; non-sectarian or a religious Quack.

Outlook on children.

Military and/or civilian service.

Outlook on Illegitimacy; adoption; perversion and homosexuality.

Outlook on sex.

Outlook on marriage.

Morals and Instincts.

Health—Shelter—Compatibility—

How to achieve the independence of each from the other?

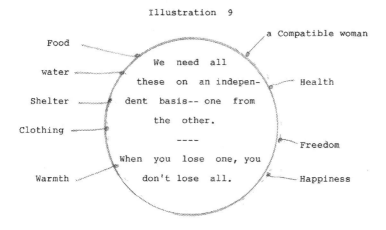

Illustration 9

Food
water
Shelter
Clothing
Warmth

a Compatible woman
Health
Freedom
Happiness

We need all these on an independent basis-- one from the other.

When you lose one, you don't lose all.

A compatible woman with----------means---------.

Health with nothing else means---------------.

Being healthy while not happy is bad.

Eating the food you enjoy in the wrong unhappy atmosphere makes it ----------.

Living in a nice house with no adequate ----------and no--------- is no good.

We should have all we could have; we cannot afford to lose one in favor of the other.

We should aim at having the most we could in good things in life. If you habituate with the wrong woman you might have trouble with the other basic items.

The Truth Versus What is Exogenous:

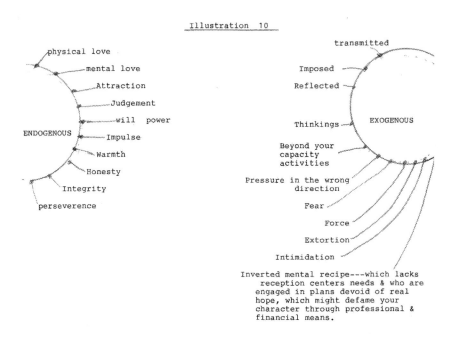

Illustration 10

physical love
mental love
Attraction
Judgement
will power
ENDOGENOUS
Impulse
Warmth
Honesty
Integrity
perseverence

transmitted
Imposed
Reflected
Thinkings — EXOGENOUS
Beyond your capacity activities
Pressure in the wrong direction
Fear
Force
Extortion
Intimidation

Inverted mental recipe---which lacks reception centers needs & who are engaged in plans devoid of real hope, which might defame your character through professional & financial means.

Resting in Sexual Difficulties After Marriage:

Are your sexual problems psychological or organic?
What would you do if that happens?

Marriage dissolution?
Masturbation?
Adultery?
Use artificial devices for your sexual pleasures?

Homosexuality?

Perversion?

Involuntary sexual activity?

Prior to marriage it would be wise to at least think about your post-marital sexual future if a difficulty arises. For example, if one partner gets sexually less capable due to disease or old age or other reasons.

Why are You Hiding Things from Each Other?

You should be confidential to each other and try not hide anything to prevent marital difficulties. It is not pleasant that knowledge should be one-sided when it is unfavorable to the other.

You should not seek incompatibility and tolerance in the wrong alley.

Forced relations based on intimidation, red tape and dishonesty should be avoided. You are in trouble when molested by the wrong woman in the face of poor legal protection due to the strong social, religious and financial states of the woman molester.

Do not submit to losing your freedom; your judgement could save you from being possessed by an incompatible woman, who offers nothing but persecution, defamation of character, character assassination and unhappiness.

Avoid a "maid habituation" deal where the main advantage is an unsatisfying sexual activity.

You never feel being a maid with a compatible woman regardless of what you do because she feels the same way and never nags about house work.

It is a constitutional right to hide things—it is actually not hiding, but there are things of a personal nature that you don't think the other person should know, because they could destroy your relations. They usually have the opposite effect and is not a healthy substitute. Trust and love go hand in hand. Do not jump into conclusions about a woman; she might be nicer or worse than you think.

Take your time and do not lump all women and all situations, that look the same, together. Man and woman are different even if they are close relations.

Is your age a problem? What is the best age? It is hard to know; it depends on how fast you mature, how well you keep your mental and physical freshness and fitness

Illustration 11

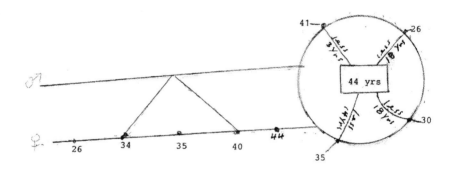

The difference in age is a private thing between the two of you if you are both over 18 years of age and understand and love each other.

Judgements and Decisions:

In matters of compatibility and love, one should have the maximum confidence in himself and make his own financial decisions. This does not mean that you should not consult and consider the advice of those whom you think are able to help you in your own ways. Avoid being a victim of religion, racial, industrial and financial quacks.

If you are not confident in yourself to make decisions, then you will be in troubles because the marriage quacks create problems for you and offer you nothing but the opposite of what you truly desire. Seek only the help of qualified people.

When you get too flexible and careless, you don't get what you want –

For beautiful sexy legs you get ugly legs.

For beautiful clean nails, you get dirty ugly nails.

For a blond, you get something else.

For sex appeal, you get sex repeal.

For sincerity, you get deceit.

For equal education and intelligence you get ignorance and lack of intellect.

For the (fill in) age, you get (fill in).

For attraction, you get repulsion.

For love you get indifference.

For physical love, you get imposed fake mental love and frigidity.

For freedom and happiness, you get confinement and misery.

For freedom of choice, you get persecuted.

For enlightening you, they blind you.

Registrations:

Marriage-wise, you are legally bound to a woman by two documents:

1) A state marriage license registered at the county clerk's office—your marriage license which you get prior to your private marriage ceremony.

2) A marriage dissolution Certificate registered at the County clerk's office—This document contains the judge's decision of restoring you to the unmarried status and things pertaining to your children and property disposition if you have any.

Chapter

13

The Difference Between Delusions and The Truth In Marriage–

Analysis of the marital status of two men calling themselves Happily Married one, is delusional, and the other one is truly happy.

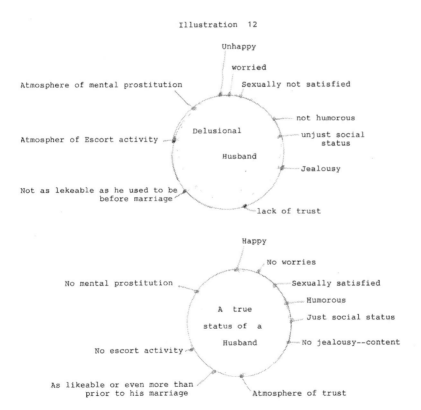

Illustration 12

Sometimes you have the wrong idea about your mate. Her thinking might be quite different than yours while you think it is the same. That is a kind of delusion and one way of cheating yourself. The problem is that sometimes (when in delusion) you have no insight into yourself and you do not know the truth about her. How are you going to discover the truth and solve your problems? Time will tell. When in doubt take your time and seek the advice from the right people.

Chapter

14

Signs of Maturity—

When a man knows that he is a man and a husband, and the woman knows that she is a woman and a wife;

When man and woman understand the sexual feelings of each other and satisfy each other sexually;

When man and woman enjoy each other the way they are;

When man and woman understand compatibility, love and respect and enjoy each other's mature outlook on life;

When man and woman understand the mechanisms of sexual intimacy from the start to the finish.

When man and woman have sound judgements and controllable will power;

When you have trust and confidence in yourself;

When you are able to make decisions in matters of independence; direction in life; professional status; engagement and marriage;

When you have certain basics in life and are able to be flexible when the need arises without injuring your basics;

To know when you are taken advantage of. The ability to be yourself and not to voluntarily engage in monkey business unsuitable for your welfare.

When you have a sense of independence and when you care about guarding your constitutional right against injustice.

To be able to put the good things you learn from others into good use for yourself and others interested in your <u>happiness</u> and well being.

Man-Woman Reactions to Each Other—

Are you uninhibited or stiff with your wife?

There are degrees of inhibition. I call stiffness as the degree of maximum inhibition.

The degree of your response depends on what you perceive from your mate by mental, visual and hearing processes.

There is a correlation between Compatibility and to what extent you lose your inhibitions with that particular woman. It is often a mutual feeling.

The more compatible you are, the less inhibited you get with all degrees in between.

Your reactions to her usually depends and is influenced by her reactions to you and vice versa. This applies to sexual and nonsexual relations.

Illustration   13

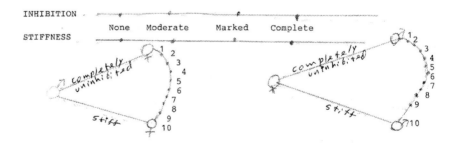

The Visible and The Invisible—

Visible	Invisible
Body	Health
Food	Love, sex, attraction
Beverages	Happiness
Shelter:	Security
House/apt./room	Fear
Money	Tolerance
Car, appliances,	Intelligence
Household goods	I.Q., Mental Capacity
Buying	Thinking
	Freedom to spend money
	Freedom to buy
	Freedom to move
	Freedom to associate
	Freedom to choose
	Knowledge
	Initiative
	Malice
	Deceit

How Do You Know You are in Love?

Your mental thinking gets concentrated on that one woman with less and less on the others.

You develop more attachment to her.

You lose your desire to be with your other girl friends the way you used to.

You care more about that one woman and think about her more often if not always.

You think she is beautiful no matter how ugly she looks in the eyes of other men.

When you touch each other it is often electrifying, at least some of the times.

Your mental, bodily and hormonal makeup react to her quite differently than to other women.

You might also have one altered degree of respiration, heart beat, temperature, depending on your age and where you are.

You cease to desire other women sexually.

You cease to mentally wonder about other women.

You like to be with that woman often if not always.

You enjoy the things she does and never get tired of being with her.

You might lose your appetite eat less especially if conditions are unfavorable. You lose weight; you lose interest in some but not all of the things you used to do, or people you used to associate with.

Keeping in mind the fact that not all loss of appetite, weight or interest in things is caused by love.

After engagement and marriage you do not change from your love before marriage. You both should make sure that you are truly in love based on adequate number of personality traits compatibility and adequate time before deciding to get engaged or to get married.

When discussing material things such as money, wills, profession your love to each other does not change. Wills, Insurance and money are delicate points in compatibility. If you have serious differences in those, then you better not get involved any further. Professional incompatibility is also a serious problem.

When you are not ashamed to expose your bodies to each other or hide certain parts of your bodies from each other for fear of losing each other e.g. she hides her legs and you hide your belly, etc.

When you feel in some way about each other with or without makeups; when you still feel the same after opening all your problems to each other.

When you do not fear discussing anything to each other.

Is Love Blind?

Love is based on the amount of knowledge fed into your senses about and from the woman you love, through sight, hearing, touch and experience.

If you do not get adequate information or if you get false information, then you would be computing on not enough knowledge for a sound judgement. It creates into a status of infatuation.

To avoid mistakes, do your matching and use your judgement after making use of your personality traits which are fed into a computer. The computer picks for those women that have personality traits compatible with yours.

No judgement is sound based solely on the computer findings. It is best to date those picked by the computer. The final decision is yours.

Is Your First Impression Always True?

The first impression is important but not always true. Give yourself some time and be conservative. Do not be blind after your first sight and your first impression. Usually not enough information is gained from first sight. Base your judgement on adequate findings.

Many women have sweet deceiving looks or too much makeup. After you get to know them better, you lose interest.

It is better to be happy than to be slap happy, on the minimum, in things such as women and money.

Choose a compatible partner that sexually satisfies you and also flavors your life with happy events. Your liberty and pursuit of happiness will not be up to par with an incompatible woman.

How can you afford to be the least important in some woman's future? The Next of Kin is something special; you don't give it to a woman. She earns it by being compatible and true to you.

Why Pick a Lower I.Q. Mate?

Things usually work better if you have close I.Q. mate, provided you have compatible personality traits. A decision on the basis of I.Q. is not desirable. You could be taken advantage of, when the smarter partner is not just or if the lower I.Q. mate is part of a mental recipe or ring engaged in ethnicity which you consider will hinder a decent family life.

I.Q., mental capacity and intellectual capabilities are not quite the same. Love and attraction does not always depend on your I.Q. Your training and experience to be a successful wife has great merits. A high I.Q. by itself does not make a perfect sexual partner. You could be very smart yet sexually maladjusted because you don't read about sex and don't expose yourself to experience it adequately.

Love—

Illustration 14

Infatuation

True
/physical
Mental
attraction

Love

Mental
not physical Transmitted
No attraction

Imposed
/resented
not physical
no attraction

46

Mental love is not based on anything you see in the woman and is not necessarily accompanied by physical love or attraction. It should be called illusion and not mental love. Physical love is usually accompanied by mental love and is based on personality traits which include attraction and sex. Sex is based on your love of the body of that woman, her sexy legs, turgidity of her body and breast, her curvature, her expressions, her beautiful face, ears, mouth, teeth, neck, bones, nails, skin, and above all her appearance during sexual intimacy.

Your sexual fitness depends on your bodily compatibility and your attitudes at the time of sexual intimacy, the stimulation of the erotic zones, the timing and the knowledge of what to do and how to handle each other from the start to the finish accompanied by a feeling of warmth and love after sex.

What is love or the love syndrome?

Love develops as a result of a combination of favorable mental, emotional, hormonal, sexual and physical factors.

When you get enough of these factors you become a "lover" with a "love syndrome". You develop a feeling of wanting to be with the woman you love. Sometimes it is very overpowering. When it overrides your judgement and will power, then you develop a problem for yourself and for her. Mutual love and sexual harmony, and satisfactions are basic items for the stability of your marriage.

The love syndrome could be pure. The degree of its integrity depends on how pure it is. It could be contaminated by exogenous transmissions or impositions to a dangerous degree. Such invasion of privacy could be injurious to your relations if it is beyond your knowledge, tolerance and mental capacity.

When in love and there is a conflict between your heart, will power and judgement, then it is best to analyze your situation further before you make a decision. Give yourself some time.

If you are single with no other problem, use your will power. It is better than exposing yourself to quackery or other kinds of racketeering.

If you don't solve your love problems to a certain extent no one else could help you much including psychiatrists and marriage councilors.

Computer matching based on your personality traits is very useful and sound if used properly and sincerely.

We use the word love in so many ways. It is best to use only when we mean it. We use the word love for sweethearts, friends or enemies. We also use it for relatives like brothers, sisters, mothers, fathers, sons and daughters. Naturally there is a great difference between the word love used for a sweetheart and the word love when you use it corresponding or talking to other relatives. In the latter case it means likeness with an emotional element categorically different from that used for your sweetheart.

When you get to meet and get acquainted with several women that you like— how are you going to analyze your situation and increase your trust to make the best choice? Perhaps you need to meet more women before wanting to be serious. Of course it depends greatly on the response of the women.

Do these women think about you the same way? Perhaps yes or not at all. Perhaps you are a one-sided dreamer at least to some of them. Your problems get solved better if you use sound criteria as shown in the diagram bellow:

	A	B	C	D	E	F	G	H
1) Mental Attraction	+	+	+	+	+	+	-	-
2) Physical Attraction	+	+	+	+	-	+	-	-
3) Judgement	-	+	-	+	+	+	-	-
4) Will Power	+	+	+	+	+	+	+	-

"F" would qualify to be the "Next of Kin" but provided she feels the same way about you.

Illustration 15

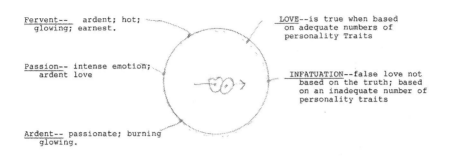

Fervent-- ardent; hot;
   glowing; earnest.

LOVE--is true when based
   on adequate numbers of
   personality Traits

Passion-- intense emotion;
   ardent love

INFATUATION--false love not
   based on the truth; based
   on an inadequate number of
   personality traits

Ardent-- passionate; burning
   glowing.

Love is basic and instinctive and we should know when we are in love. We also know when. We do know. When you feel you are in love you tell her you are in love, but you should know that she is in love too before you tell her so.

How do you know she is in love? You know from her behavior and reactions but you never really know until she tells you so. Would you take it as so, if you do not feel you know her enough or when you don't have enough to go by to know if she is sincere? You just have to use your judgement. Mistakes are made and will always be made.

When you are in love, you gradually catch up on each other. It gets to be catchy. Your behavior towards each other becomes more stable and adaptive in some ways.

Love is a pausing thing your mate feels it, however it could be faked but not for long. It is a coordinated mental, hormonal, physical and emotional complex based on what you perceive from the love through sight, hearing and touch. Love is an entity based on perception of visible and invisible things which are compatible to your wellbeing.

Engagement and Marriage—

Most of us do not plunge into these things unless we are in love. If we do them there is room for improving ourselves perhaps after making mistakes.

It is unfavorable to be engaged to a woman even if she loves you when her mind wanders and has room for other men. Certainty is a must for such an important and serious relation.

Love based purely on mental perception is not a sure thing and could be imposed, transmitted and not based on compatible personality traits. It is an infatuation, if it is not accompanied by attraction and sexual harmony. There is much less chance for mind wandering in a relation based on true attraction and on sexual compatibility than on mental love shrouded by uncertainty with no sound physical fulfillment. Mental love is in the realm of delusion when you do not enjoy a satisfying sexual relation; you do not enjoy the company of this woman in public. When you are at social gatherings you just feel there is something missing in her that does not qualify her to be your wife or the "Next of Kin" and people notice these things.

Afterall what is mental love when it is imposed to cover up for all the other inadequacies you are suffering from.

Mind Wandering–

Is when your mind wanders and you start thinking about other women. This happens at any time even during sexual intimacy, which could lead to sexual dissatisfaction with your mate. Mind wandering could be real, imposed or transmitted, transient and harmless or serious leading to marital troubles and dissolution.

Why would your mind wander?

When your wife does not possess what is ideal for you such as sexy slim, beautiful thighs, legs, feet, hands, beauty of her face, teeth, hair, eyes, her response to stimulation and the manner of her sexual behavior during intercourse and after. When she is not as capable of making love to you as you are to her.

Mind wandering is a very sensitive factor in compatibility. When your mind does not wander it is a very nice sign of compatibility. The degree of wandering is perhaps proportional to the degree of compatibility.

GRAPHIC ILLUSTRATION:

Mind Wandering   > <u>0 degrees of MAXIMUM</u>
Sexual Satisfaction > <u>MAXIMUM degrees of 0</u>
Compatibility   > <u>MAXIMUM degrees of MNIIMUM</u> (or none)

She Lost Interest—

Some women are interested in men on an unequal basis. When you pursue a status of equality she loses interest in you and leaves you after starting troubles either directly or indirectly in a way blaming you for it. Other women lose interest for other reasons. You and your children suffer as a result by losing certain instinctive or acquired pleasures. You are secondary to your income to many women and it is pleasurable to have your income and sometimes it is more pleasurable to have it without having the nuisance of having you around.

If she cannot control your income you could face income paralysis if she manages losing that.

A woman also could lose interest in you if she cannot use you for mental recipe purposes to promote the welfare of some against the welfare of other to your disadvantage. Avoid women who lose interest in you when things are to your advantage for a serious relationship.

Love and Marriage

Is your marriage going in the right direction? Are you happy? Content perhaps not if you have cheated? Your conscience about some instinctive things in that will bother you the rest of your life regardless. Neglecting sensitive things in you as far as making a decision for marriage, often leads to troubles when these things are or are not brought up to the surface.

If you like marrying a Virgin you probably cannot stay happy with a mate used to premarital intercourse, or if she was a homosexual or a pervert, or if she enjoys sexual relations outside marriage.

If she is of a different religion or a different race than you prefer or she loves to engage in social and religious quarreling.

A cardinal sign in compatibility is when the man and woman can maturely stimulate each other to the fullest attaining the maximum in sexual enjoyment and satisfaction. Time and the degree of stimulation are the most important factors to attain normal orgasm and usual ejaculation.

A compatible couple are the ones that truly love to stimulate each other to the fullest. It is based on what they percept from each other. Thy believe they are worth the stimulation therefore they attain maximum joy and satisfaction. Each percepts potent sexual impulses from the other, which are converted and transmitted as smooth psycho-sexual impulses of the highest quality for a best sexual relation.

If you do not believe your partner is worth stimulating to the fullest you know for sure that you are heading for an incompatible relation to start with. This is especially true if the man feels that way because by not stimulating the woman to the fullest she will not achieve orgasm and hence maximum sexual satisfaction. The woman has to be the same way, otherwise she will be acting frigid which is sexually unsatisfying and irritating to the man. If you both do not feel your stimulation comes from love and is sincere, then you are laboring and straining yourself to achieve what you are not maturely capable of doing for each other.

Some women are sexually compatible and you love to have a relation with them. However when it comes to appearing with them in public you do not feel the same way. A more compatible woman is the one that has both qualities and you would love to be identified with her in public. She also possesses the qualities that are most satisfying to you sexually and your feelings are mutual.

Mind wandering could be a serious problem especially at times of sexual intimacy.

SEX— is a very important quality for marriage. It is a reflection of the female qualities that qualify her to be the "Next of Kin".

When she is sexually beautiful and satisfying to you, it means her other qualities are up to your taste and happiness.

Marriage not based on sex is not sound and is not healthy because sex is the cream of the essential qualities in a woman. Sex is a reflection of the womanly love, attraction, beauty, eroticism, intelligence, character and other compatible personality traits. Sexual compatibility is the result of combining physical and mental love and attraction into a harmonious psychosexual and neurovascular reactions.

Love is the result of the melting of all the qualities the woman possesses that are transmitted and precepted by you.

SEX leads to true love which leads to a life of enjoyable sexual relations which improves practically all aspects of our life.

To understand and enjoy sex more fully you should continuously try to improve your knowledge of sex and try to understand each other sexually, explore your erotic zones and improve your methods of foreplay, execution and timing.

Foreplay is vital for a sound sexual relation. For example if you do not have proper foreplay for about at least 20 minutes, your psychosexual impulses do not operate to the fullest and your ejaculation and her orgasm are not as good as you want them to be, hence not enough satisfaction.

Erotic Zones of The Body—

Man and woman have erotic zones for their sexual enjoyments and pleasures. Some are natural like the glans penis and the clitoris. The mind is erotic. The outer genitals are erotic.

In man— the glans penis is erotic, also the lips, tongue, ears, neck, and nipples.

In woman—the clitoris is the most erotic organ. The whole vulval region is erotic including the outer portion of the vagina and perhaps the middle third at least in some. Also, the nipples, ears, neck, loins, thighs, legs, wrists, palms and tips of fingers.

Sexual excitation could result from vision, touch, sound and of course the mind can get you sexually excited through thinking and perception.

Men and women could get sexually excited by the sight of person of the opposite sex. The degree varies with the degree of sex appeal.

Sex, eroticism and will power go hand in hand so that we could enjoy things at the proper time or delay the timing because of adversities.

The intensity of your sexual response and your will power to suppress your psychosexual urges when you have to, varies. Being very sexy does not make you improper when you have adequate will power to suppress your psychosexual impulses when you are not in the right place to be completely uninhibited on a mutual basis. The intensity of your sexual desires and how proper you are do go hand in hand.

Fertility—

A man is called fertile when his semen contains sperms capable of penetrating and fertilizing a healthy ovum—a process that leads to conception of a healthy baby.

A woman is called fertile when she ovulates and produces healthy ova capable of accepting the penetration of a healthy sperm that initiates a process leading to the conception of a healthy baby.

A man and a woman could be fertile by virtue of possessing normal semen and normal ova. Yet one or both of them may be sterile because the avenues to conception are blocked by disease or the timing of intercourse is not during ovulation. This creates what we call sterility problems.

Fertility and Sterility Studies—

When a couple have difficulties of not having children, they usually seek the advice of an expert physician, in the field, who examines both and carries fertility and sterility studies on both.

MALE FERTILITY STUDIES INCLUDE IF NEEDED—

1) Semen analysis: the semen is considered abnormal if the volume is below 1.5 ml or -5ml per ejaculation or if the sperm count is below 20 million/ml or if the % of abnormal sperm is +20% and if sperm mobility is poor. Other studies are also done such as the degree of sperm mobility in the endocrinal plug of women.

2) Testicular biopsy for microscopic examinations.

3) Endocrinal studies: the thyroid the pituitary and the saliva glands.

FEMALE FERITILITY STUDIES—

1) Age of the female – is she ovulating?
2) Exfoliative cytology, cervical smears; Endocrinal biopsy.
3) Cervical mucous plug studies—degree of
   a) sperm mobility and penetration;
   b) abnormal endocrinal secretions.
4) Endocrinal or fallopian tubes blockage studies.

SEX CHROMOSOME STUDIES OF BOTH IF INDICATED—

Nuclear sex abnormalities are looked for in humid buccal and cervical smears; sometimes studies are done on leucocytes schisms, etc. This is not considered routine procedure.

Frigidity—could cause infertility problems meaning sterility by virtue of poor timing of the intercourse time to coincide with the time of ovulation.

The sperms reach their destination but there is no ova to fertilize. Frigidity could also cause ejaculation outside the vagina, so the ovum will not have sperm to fertilize her.

Other tests are also done such as serology blood and urine examinations and prostatic biopsy etc.

Hyperthyroidism, diabetes mellitus and peptic ulcers also could decrease fertility in women.

Contraception – Means Birth Control–

You could achieve birth control by many ways. The most common way now is oral contraception—the woman takes the "pills" on a schedule. These pills are made of hormones: a combination of ESTROGEN and PROGESTERONE. The amount of these two hormones in the "pills" varies depending on the company manufacturing the pills. The physician usually prescribes the "pill" which has the most suitable combination as to amount of the hormones to that particular woman depending on her examination. Not all women take the same kind of "pill". Some are best suited for one kind, while others are best suited for another kind.

There are other methods of artificial contraception (with control) such as using INTERUTERINE Devices (IUD). Jellies, diaphragms, lozenges, douches etc.

Surgical ligation of the fallopian tubes in the female and of the vasa differentia (the tubes that transmit sperms—semen—from the testes to the seminal vesicles) in the male.

The "Pill"–for oral contraception (with control):

When you take a "pill" so frequently and for a long time to make you enjoy your sexual life with your mate, it would be a good idea for you to learn—what could the "pill" do to you after you take it?

The doctor will tell you whether you are suited to take the "pill".

Some women develop what we call "side effects" after taking the "pill". Sometimes it takes years for some of these side effects to develop. If you know what these side effects are then if they develop in you, you will recognize them in time and you report them to your doctor who might tell you to stop the "pill". Your doctor usually tells you of these side effects. Considering the vast number of women taking the "pill" the frequency of the side effects are rare.

SIDE EFFECTS OF ORAL CONTRACEPTIVE PILLS'

1) If you miss two periods in a row;
2) If you do not tolerate the "Pill";
3) Change in weight—gain or loss;
4) Change in your skin—condition of the skin of your face; skin yellowing or rashes; acne, greasy skin & hair;
5) Yellowing of the eyes;
6) Unusual swelling—fluid retention;
7) Change in hair such as loss of scalp hair or increase in body hair;
8) Change in libido (sexual desire)—decrease or increase;
9) Breast tenderness;
10) Abnormal vaginal and cervical pap smears; spotting or vaginal bleeding;
11) Mental depression;
12) Menstrual changes, Tension, irritability, irregularities & poise;
13) Gastric disturbances; nausea and vomiting;
14) Leg and abdominal cramps;
15) Blood clotting in veins such as your Varicose Veins or in your lungs or brain vessels give you signs and symptoms:
    a) Leg veins clots cause leg pains.
    b) Lung clots dcause chest pains and coughing of blood.
    c) Brain clots cause dizziness, blurred vision & severe headache.

16) Your blood sugar and lipid levels might increase.

The doctor usually checks if you have epilepsy, diabetes, high blood pressure, heart disease, kidney disease, migraine, asthma, fibrosis, etc., before he decides whether you should take the "pill". He may advise not to take the "pill" if you have cancer of the breast or uterus or serious liver disease or undiagnosed vaginal bleeding.

Chapter

20

Sexual Decline After Marriage:

When the main reason for marriage was not for true love;

Sexual enjoyment and having children on a solid family style basis.

When love was false, only a channel, a beautiful deceit act to get to the first stage of the game of getting ahead labelled marriage.

Once the legal solution is established then love and sex are no longer needed or important. Sex becomes an instrument of persecution-----or else no sex. Frigidity, false or true, dominates the marriage life when things are not up to par. Things become beyond capacity which ends in marriage dissolution.

Hishiar Shamdin

Impotence:

Illustration 16

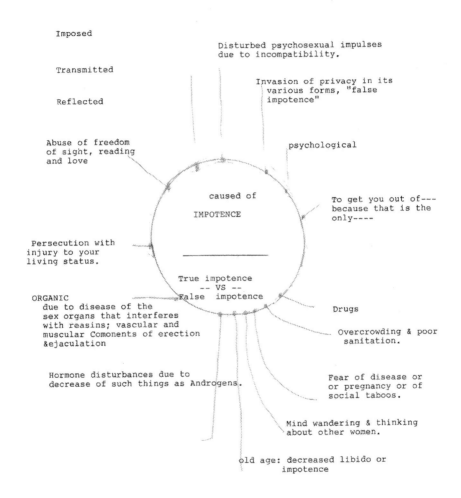

IMPOTENCE

Imposed

Transmitted

Reflected

Disturbed psychosexual impulses
due to incompatibility.

Invasion of privacy in its
various forms, "false
impotence"

Abuse of freedom
of sight, reading
and love

psychological

caused of

IMPOTENCE

To get you out of---
because that is the
only----

Persecution with
injury to your
living status.

True impotence
-- VS --
False impotence

ORGANIC
due to disease of the
sex organs that interferes
with reasins; vascular and
muscular Comonents of erection
&ejaculation

Drugs

Overcrowding & poor
sanitation.

Hormone disturbances due to
decrease of such things as Androgens.

Fear of disease or
or pregnancy or of
social taboos.

Mind wandering & thinking
about other women.

old age: decreased libido or
impotence

Illustration 17

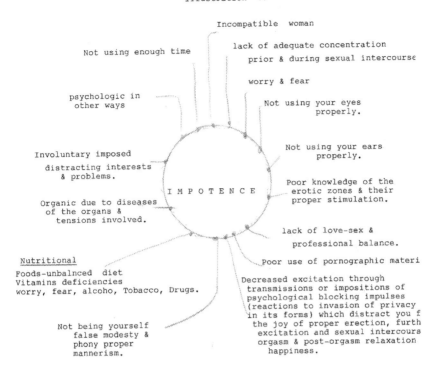

Incompatible woman

lack of adequate concentration
prior & during sexual intercourse

Not using enough time

worry & fear

psychologic in
other ways

Not using your eyes
properly.

Not using your ears
properly.

Involuntary imposed
distracting interests
& problems.

I M P O T E N C E

Poor knowledge of the
erotic zones & their
proper stimulation.

Organic due to diseases
of the organs &
tensions involved.

lack of love-sex &
professional balance.

Nutritional
Foods-unbalnced diet
Vitamins deficiencies
worry, fear, alcoho, Tobacco, Drugs.

Poor use of pornographic materi

Decreased excitation through
transmissions or impositions of
psychological blocking impulses
(reactions to invasion of privacy
in its forms) which distract you f
the joy of proper erection, furth
excitation and sexual intercours
orgasm & post-orgasm relaxation
happiness.

Not being yourself
false modesty &
phony proper
mannerism.

Professional indulgence, concentration wise and time wise to the point of losing interest in your girlfriend, fiancée, sweetheart or wife: the wife should have at least an equal importance as your profession at least as to time to make your solutions more enjoyable, lack of balance between your profession and your home life indicates some kind of incompatibility. Elements of age, desire and other factors should be considered.

To learn how to avoid distractions and how to balance your life is a cure for some kinds of impotence when it is psychological or due to fatigue. Your status should need a great deal of improvement of your tolerance to each other is limited to the period of sexual intimacy only.

Mental deviation at the time or before sexual intimacies through creating unpleasant moods by such acts as nagging; being sarcastic about how you spend your time; how little your accomplishments are; how bad your eating habits are ; how terrible you are sexually compared with other men she knew; how poor is your knowledge of foreplay; how fast and uncontrollable is your orgasm; your poor knowledge of her erotic zones and how rough you are in stimulating them.

By nagging she deflates your ego; deflates your psychosexual impulses which of course deviates you from wanting to make love to her.

There are many ways of injuring your psychosexual impulses by associating with an incompatible woman: accusations; taking sides with others; poor knowledge of sex; escort activities ; mental prostitution and the use of sex for other purposes.

Chapter 91

How Can You Make Mistakes in Finding A Compatible Woman?

When you erroneously think that she is thinking as decent as you are when she is not. When you mistake an instrument for an individual.

When you labor to make her compatible when she is not.

If she has a double personality.

When both of you have different basics in life.

If you are non-sectarian and she is engaged in Communion or quackery.

Rigidity with no basics.

Too much rigidity when not in conflict with your basics.

When you don't feel secure together.

Lack of faith in each other.

Lack of trust and suspiciousness.

Superior attitudes—when it is not visible.

Lack of feelings for each other's basics.

A purely materialistic and commercial relationship.

When you have got yourself an investigator instead of a wife.

When you are in for love and she is in for malice; deceit; grudge; inclinations for injuries to you and to others in your category. Such situation should not be legalized to be called "the Next of Kin".

Creations of atmospheres of air pollution; escort activity, mental

prostitution & brain washing instead of a healthy compatible atmosphere which is stimulating physically, mentally & professionally.

When you cannot recognize each other in a crowd.

When you cannot achieve meetings of the minds.

Compatibility VS Incompatibility—

WHAT IS ON THE MIND?

You have to lower yourself to see that. Why not have her move higher herself to see me?

You have to lose your license to lower yourself to that. Why not her get a license to get to you? Wouldn't that be better?

You have to have more money to please her. She will not give you a pass unless you do, e.g. break your spirit first. You have to escape before she does it to you.

So you could imagine from the above there is a gap in your situation, therefore incompatible situations to start with.

Signs of Incompatibility—

Frigidity, nagginess, adultery, perversion, homosexuality. Persecution personalities:

a) Racial; b. Religious; c. Sexual; d. Financial; e. professional; f. Familial; g. Any combinations of the above; I. Others; j. hostage activities; k. Investigating activities; l. Invasion of your constitutional rights.

Mental recipe take-over with professional deviation and eliminating you inadvertently into a "maid status". Temporary or permanent unnecessary irritations.

Jealousy and tampering.

Creating family and religious problems through quackery.

Magnify meetings and create problems when around.

Tampering with your incentive and judgement.

Create fear situation.

Hide virtues and magnify false faults.

Punishment for moments of happiness and humor.

Dominance of a 'Monkey type of personality' over your private affairs in your leisure time.

Lack of insight into your rates of husband and wife.

Superiority and Inferiority complex practices—submission she is ahead; you are not; she is your guardian; see how that feels; for the same reason you leave to do the dishes next time; you have to cook next time etc. as the alternative.

Lack of harmony in your buying tastes; inferior decorating; type of cloth you wear and the way you spend money.

Different outlook on children; pets; old and new things—(housing, car, furniture, appliances, clothing, books, etc.); colors; music; friends; associates; social events; drinking; smoking; drugs; dancing; vacationing; income; wills; doctors; dentists; where to buy things; Insurance; lawyers; Bank accounts; who should handle the budget; relations to your other relatives; religion; loans; charge accounts; buy; lease; rent; membership in clubs etc.

When competing with your profession for love, either she or your profession, she cannot tolerate you in your present Profession.

When there is no interest to buy the things you like such as buying a new house. You have to fix an old house or live in a trailer etc.

When she is not sexually understanding and harmonious, she likes to use her sex to an advantage to get other things at least beyond reason.

When a woman's cause overrides her status as a wife with no time for sex, no mood for sex, no time for leisure, etc,

When you have got yourself a job as a maid and you have to look for a wife.

Interferes with your reading and thinking habits. Interferes with your happy habits.

Develops personality disorders in you.

Lack of awareness of what makes you happy.

Disregard for your happiness in favor of her projects and ambitions.

When she is professionally injurious through her conduct and associates.

When she has a persecution complex; she likes to persecute herself to persecute others.

Lack of interest in doing things together such as going to movies, dances, shows, driving out, visit friends etc,

Lack of mutual purpose and timing for doing things.

Having an attitude that will get you into trouble with your other relatives and friends.

Some Basic Incompatible Points—

Illustration 18

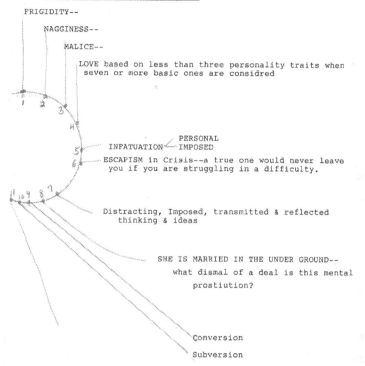

SOME BASIC INCOMPATIBLE POINTS--

FRIGIDITY--

NAGGINESS--

MALICE--

LOVE based on less than three personality traits when seven or more basic ones are considred

PERSONAL
INFATUATION----IMPOSED

ESCAPISM in Crisis--a true one would never leave you if you are struggling in a difficulty.

Distracting, Imposed, transmitted & reflected thinking & ideas

SHE IS MARRIED IN THE UNDER GROUND-- what dismal of a deal is this mental prostiution?

Conversion

Subversion

Investigating for-----
Mental recipe activities.

It is too much for a woman to ask for love, devotion, trust, equality and confidence when she prctices deceit, malice, takes & no give, one may. Communication and abuse of your decency and persecution fro ----

Is This A Compatible Female Behavior?

Eggs wanted for breakfast—you get oat meal.

Steak wanted for lunch, no you get three eggs and so on.

You want to buy a new house, she arranges to buy an old house.

You want a new car, she buys an old car, a different model and a color you don't like.

If you are a doctor, never invites doctors' wives, only other wives.

You want nice curtains for the windows, she prefers to hang unattractive stuff.

You get a size 11&1/2 C shoe from her, when your shoe size is 9 or 13. You get size 40 underwear when you are size 36.

You get a size 14-34 shirt when your size is 15-1/2 –32.

You get colored towels when you want white ones. If you want colored ones you get the wrong colors.

You come home to have dinner at 5 P.M. You see her cleaning her room or the kitchen or painting her toes or shampooing her hair.

When you want to go out for dinner she goes out with this person or that person, so you can't go when you want.

She gets on the telephone when you need it most. When it is time for love she is at her neighbor's; or when she is home she is untouchable, everything hurts or is tender.

She is always glad that it is over.

When you are in the mood she disturbs your psychosexual impulses by starting to nag or by inviting escorts to do that for her.

It is time for coffee which you have been drinking all day.

23

What is More Important You or Your Money?

Illustration 19
What is more important: You or your $?

Diagramatic:

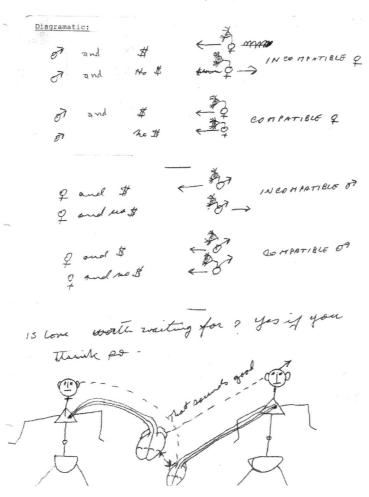

♂ and #

♂ and No $ INCOMPATIBLE ♀

♂ and $

♂ no #   COMPATIBLE ♀

♀ and #

♀ and no $ INCOMPATIBLE ♂

♀ and $

♀ and no $ COMPATIBLE ♂

IS love worth waiting for ? yes if you think so -

That sounds good

Illustration 19

SHE LOST INTEREST	VS	SHE CHANGED HER MIND
He is on welfare	-----	She lost interest.
He moved to	-----	She changed her mind.
He has money	-----	She changed her mind.
He lost his	-----	She lost interest.
He does not have a job	-----	She lost interest.
He does not like pets in the house	-----	She lost interest.
He looked down on	-----	She lost interest
He looked up on	-----	She changed her mind.
He reacted to	-----	She lost interest.
He did not do the	-----	She lost interest.
He did not bring	-----	She lost interest.
He got a nerve to	-----	She changed her mind
He did not pay enough attention to ...	-----	She lost interest.
He did not donate to	-----	She changed her mind.
He did not buy	-----	She lost interest.
He reacted to her	-----	She lost interest.
He did not write to	-----	She lost interest.
He did not pay	-----	She changed her mind.
He did not respond to	-----	She lost interest.
He threw her	-----	She lost interest.
He has ......on his	-----	She changed her mind.
His relatives........	-----	She changed her mind.
He turned down.......	-----	She lost interest.
He is sexy.	-----	She changed her mind.
He wants to get married	-----	She changed her mind.
He is too serious	-----	She lost interest.

If your basics are not protected then you are in trouble, mentally, physically and sexually. X-s, mental recipes and incompatibles, when operating in rings can do great injustice to male-female compatibility.

Her Reasons To Be With That Man – True or False:

Because—of one or a combination of more than one:

> He makes his bed every morning
> He does his own dishes.
> He is a good cook
> He cleans the house
> He is rich
> He is neat
> His hobbies are up to her taste
> His profession is interesting to her
> He has some ....and...........
> He takes the garbage out
> He used to be a................
> He likes to eat.................
> He used to have a...........
> He used to be in.............
> He did not mind to.........before..........
> She is getting tired of working,
> She needs some of his money.
> He is easily influenced..
> He enjoys picking at and nag at.
> He is O.K. to insult, it is good for her ego.

She likes to make that man work hard even on weekends and vacations— do the gardening; the...........; and the...........

She is mentally and physically in love and it is up to par to her judgement and will power. It does not interfere with her personal independence and flexibility, is not professionally injurious to her constitutional rights; not injurious emotionally and or sexually, not submissive; not injurious to others; there is no racial and religious quackery; does not encourage escort activities and mental prostitution and above all has a flavor of privacy and sexual content, and the feeling that you are truly loved and wanted.

Can You Explain What The Following Questions Mean To You?

> you have to ....see that?
> you have to be...........to.........that?
> you have to ....to.......?
> you have............the alternative?

It all depends on what you have in words to fill the dotted spaces in the questions asked.

They are perhaps different than what I had in mind at the time I wrote this book.

How can you relate these questions and answers to male-female compatibility?

What could happen if you are married to an incompatible (something is missing)—?

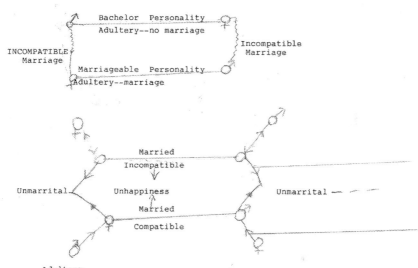

Illustration 20

What Could Happen If You Are Married To An Incompatible
(Something Is Missing)--?

Adultery
Mate Swapping
Social uneasiness
Employment difficulties or good employment.
Marital difficulties--Jealousy, irritations,
    impotence, peronality problems, violence etc.
Marriage dissolution.

Adultery

Mate swapping

Social outcast

Employment difficulties or good employment,

Marital difficulties—jealousy, irritations, impotence, personality problems, violence etc.

Marriage dissolution.

Compatibility-Incompatibility Situations-Diagramatic

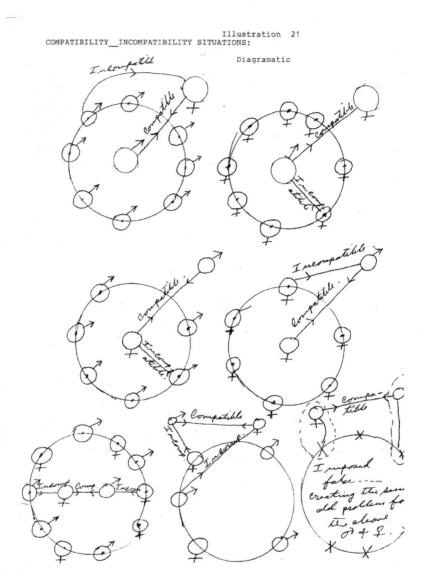

Illustration 21
COMPATIBILITY__INCOMPATIBILITY SITUATIONS:

Diagramatic

Problems in Male-Female Compatibility—Diagramatic

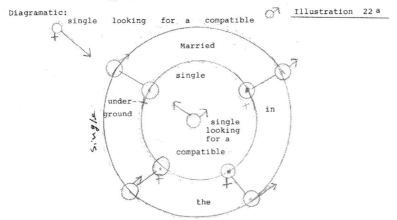

PROBLEMS IN MALE - FEMALE COMPATIBILITY-

Diagramatic:
single looking for a compatible ♂   Illustration 22 a

Married

single

under-
ground   in

single
looking
for a
compatible

the

Married in the underground is one of the sources of escort activities;
mental prostiution; frigidity; crimes; settled in the
underground activities and marriage dissolutions.

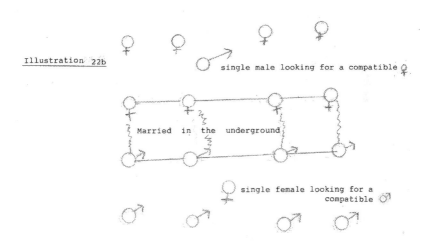

Illustration 22b

single male looking for a compatible ♀

Married in the underground

single female looking for a
compatible ♂

Illustration 23

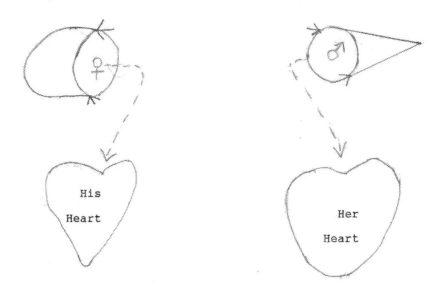

Diagram illustrating the ♂ and the ♀ feeling each
others heart, a sign of compatibility; however
it could be transmitted or imposed; it should b
accompanied by other criteria of compatibility
and be something constant.

24

What Lacks in Incompatibility?

There is a lack of what a man needs in a companion, to be wife or a wife. The same thing applies to a woman in what she wants in a man.

If the relations are not based on love and sex, then it must be defective as compatible situation based on personality traits.

Such relations are not a "Next of Kin" relations in the true sense of the word.

It is in the category of Income providing, Business, Investment, Investigation; Conversion; the need for that type of progeny for specific reasons; or for industrial, religious of subversive reasons not in the best interest of one of the partners.

Man needs a woman for sexual intimacy. Masturbation; sex services; pornography and perversion are no substitutes.

It should be a man's or woman's decision as to who they want for a partner. The more knowledge and more experience you acquire, the better decision you make.

The use of computers, legal and scientific advice should not replace our true judgement and will power. One should be helped and forced to make a decision.

How to overcome adversity by another person who is close personality wise or is a relative?

How to smear one through smearing another person?

Illustration 24

How to smear indirectly by smearing another person .

who is close personality-wise or is a relative ?

How to smear one through smearing another person?

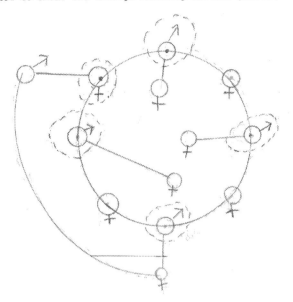

A diagramatic analysis of how Quacks tackle persons of
similar personality traits.

What happens in incompatibility ? You get deviated from a better life,
liberty and pursuit of happiness. Deviation from comfort to
discomfort; you get busy in unpleasant circles--see how this
feels! See how that feels! See ....see........To test his
reaction to.........; response to......; one way mental recipe....

Diagrammatic analysis of how quacks tackle persons of similar personality traits.

What happens in incompatibility? You get deviated from a better life, liberty and pursuit of happiness. Deviation from comfort to discomfort; you get busy in unpleasant hurdles.

In sex for instance: how this feels! See how that feels! See .... See .....see To test his reaction to......; response to ....; one way mental recipe....... .

Channeling a person to marry somebody he does not think is compatible is a poor practice with bad consequences to everybody. It is not a good example for others to follow. The results are personality disorders and unhappiness.

Why do you develop personality disorders in an incompatible situation?

What does Quackery testing your progeny mean? How does that bring happiness?

What does "second class in a mental recipe" means?

What is false love? False happiness? False compatibility? False.........?

When caught in an incompatible situation then you might get busy with: is this the same? Is that the same? Is this better than..........? See why? See how that feels? You become the target of defamation of character, character assassination; intimidation; to protect you and take care of you with Quackery.

What does the Compatible Election mate mean? What does the Incompatible Election mate mean?

What does reconciliation quackery mean? What does it mean "to get you over your problem" in the wrong alley mean?

How can the X's and/or Quacks abuse your Constitutional rights visibly and/or invisibly after final marriage dissolution (divorce).

How does incompatibility undermine your voting rights; your city residence; your state residency; your faith in your country and your citizenship?

How can you avoid an injurious flexibility in your relations with the woman you love?

How can you analyze a situation when, for example, a woman goes out with other men, but would not go out with you, unless you are engaged to her? Or she has sexual relations with others freely, but when it comes to you she has to be engaged?

Is it bad to have your independence? Professional integrity and wellbeing is tied up to your relations to a Certain mate, Compatible or not.

We should have personal security and independence, which we should not lose when the other mate decides to leave. How can a person overcome his problems semantically? Is this always possible?

Clicking Into Destruction of Marriage—

YOU CANNOT BLAME YOUR TROUBLES SOLELY ON OTHERS. YOU ARE BOTH ADULTS AND ARE THE LEGAL PILLARS FOR IT.

We should mention that it is a pity that a fairly true love should be destroyed and terminate in a marriage dissolution on the basis of mental upheaval due to :

1) Racism with you indirectly involved in it or not at all, just the other Quack;
2) Envelopment in religious quackery;
3) Envelopment in secret societies' Quackery;
4) Envelopment in subversion through marriage.

Love based on solid grounds and both partners have mentality to understand and cope with what is coming is in good shape. If you do not engage in the above four, then you have nothing to worry about.

Stalling—

When there is stalling in everything you do, then it is best to find your way out of the circle where there is nothing but stuffing your mind with unpleasant things. When you stay in that circle then you would be wasting your time with such things as:

> He lost such and such;
> That talk is antisemitic;
> That was the reason.
> See why?
> See how that feels?
> For the same reason!
> To protect him.
> Picked.
> They know that.
> He knows that.
> She knows that.
> He/she told so and so about him.
> You tough (or other) on so and so.
> That is (dumb or other).

Chapter

25

Sources of Troubles to Your Compatibility—

DIAGRAMATIC—

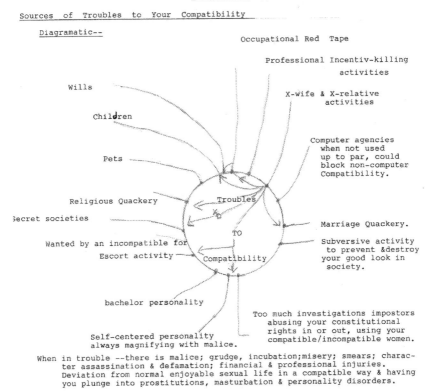

Illustration 25

Sources of Troubles to Your Compatibility

Diagramatic--

Occupational Red Tape

Professional Incentiv-killing
activities

Wills

X-wife & X-relative
activities

Children

Computer agencies
when not used
up to par, could
block non-computer
Compatibility.

Pets

Troubles

Religious Quackery

Secret societies

TO

Marriage Quackery.

Wanted by an incompatible for

Subversive activity
to prevent &destroy
your good look in
society.

Escort activity

Compatibility

bachelor personality

Too much investigations impostors
abusing your constitutional
rights in or out, using your
compatible/incompatible women.

Self-centered personality
always magnifying with malice.

When in trouble --there is malice; grudge, incubation;misery; smears; character assassination & defamation; financial & professional injuries.
Deviation from normal enjoyable sexual life in a compatible way & having
you plunge into prostitutions, masturbation & personality disorders.

When in trouble there is malice; grudge; incubation; misery; smears; character assassination & defamation; financial and

professional injuries. Deviation from normal enjoyable sexual life
that is compatible, can plunge you into prostitutions, masturbation
and personality disorders.

Acclamatization to Unreasonable Nuisance—

WHAT IS TOO MUCH TO BEAR?

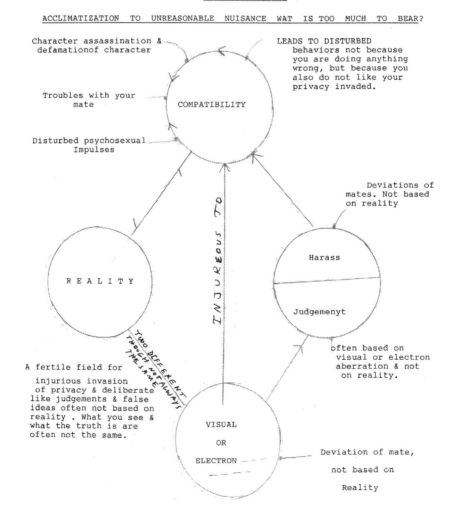

Illustration 26

ACCLIMATIZATION TO UNREASONABLE NUISANCE WAT IS TOO MUCH TO BEAR?

Character assassination &
defamationof character

LEADS TO DISTURBED
behaviors not because
you are doing anything
wrong, but because you
also do not like your
privacy invaded.

Troubles with your
mate

COMPATIBILITY

Disturbed psychosexual
Impulses

Deviations of
mates. Not based
on reality

INJUREOUS TO

REALITY

Harass

Judgemenyt

TWO DIFFERENT
THOUGH NOT ALWAYS
THE SAME

often based on
visual or electron
aberration & not
on reality.

A fertile field for
injurious invasion
of privacy & deliberate
like judgements & false
ideas often not based on
reality . What you see &
what the truth is are
often not the same.

VISUAL

OR

ELECTRON

Deviation of mate,

not based on

Reality

What Could Happen if for example a Doctor Marries an Incompatible Woman?

A very irritating life, sometimes intolerable, burns out the Capacity of most people. You get involved in all kinds of freedom fixing solutions, such as loans made against your will and professional injuries and pestering. Also, you get to be the target of red tape beyond your Constitutional right. There are all kinds of limitations and fixation of your rights and character e.g. defamation of character; character assassination and financial difficulties that might eat into your professional integrity,

Also, meddling with your professional way of life through financial troubles, creation of group hostilities against you. "You suffer and she and/or the progeny collects; but never you".

A man and a woman from different mental recipes could be compatible and happy if they have enough personality traits of similar mature and flexible enough as to override and not interfere with their mental recipe attachments.

Marriage—is not an easy decision to make, especially after you have failed one or more times. To be honest and make a sincere decision will save us a lot of troubles, which we could afford to be without. Use your personal experience which you have gained after you have failed in your first or previous marriages. You could make use of computer personality traits matching; Certified neat characters; marriage Councilors; Doctors; Psychiatrists; Experience of relatives and friends; Books and Magazines, etc.

Get married because you have found the right compatible mate, not because if it does not work you could always get a divorce- (marriage dissolution).

In the Practice of Medicine, Doctors could experience many unpleasant things —

Fear; demoralization; degradation; grudge; jealousy; Intimidations by direct or indirect means; unreasonable harassing by those not experienced enough in the field of investigations; Quack patients trying to make extra money by suing the Doctors.

Wives using patients for malpractice suits, because they have failed to get their husbands' wills or control on his finances; adverse social situations when the Doctor has to wait to be sick before he could find a practice or when you find a practice others have found ways of legalizing how to spend your money.

She Is In To Compete With You and To Win Approval—
Do You Call That True Love? It is Best to
Make These Women Understand That
We are Looking For Compatibles.

She becomes your wife to compete with you, not to be part of you and to enjoy life with you. She is your wife solely to prove that she is better than you. She directly or indirectly magnifies your faults and hides hers behind you or creates bigger ones for you than hers. She becomes a monster in reflecting her inadequacies on you. She is in to prove that you are no good and everything that goes on wrong is your fault.

She is in to criticize you and help you the wrong way, at the wrong time for the wrong reason at your own expense. She might be in just to win your approval once you do that and say she is O.K., nice, beautiful etc. She pulls the rug from under you, creates more troubles and leaves.

The Indifferent Woman Who Lacks Insight
Into Her Status of Being Wife—

When you marry a mental recipe woman, you really have a problem of not yet having a wife. You have just made a questionable decision and have legalized invasion of your privacy. Your future in life becomes uncertain as to your goals.

A true wife is not a mental recipe practitioner ; she is an independent individual like you. She is in for love and not deceit; mental prostitution; and escort activity.

The indifferent woman does not know her role as a wife and lacks interest in it. When she has problems, she would rather consult others than her husband. Every thing you do impinges on her freedom; she likes to do things you don't like; invite, buy and cook what is irritating to you. A way of cornering and irritating yourself in the wrong alley.

What Do You Inherit Through Marriage To an Incompatible Woman?

Malcontent. Escort activities operating in rings with your finance or wife or the former girl friend or escorts operating on their own. Revenge for the decision through mental prostitution, brain washing and other avenues of disturbing the peace.

Invasion of Privacy Through Her.

She is married in the underground. Escort societies troubles; Racial and religious Quackery—you find yourself married to a ring instead of a wife.

Marriage counselling versus Marriage Quackery—

I have no fixed ideas about marriage counseling. If you both have Confidence based on knowledge and experience, then gook luck.

If you both feel that marriage Counseling impinges on your freedom, then you should seek some other avenues of help.

Marriage Counseling becomes more difficult if your backgrounds, race, religion, culture, occupation and national origin are different, of course. This depends on the degree of difference and on how liberal or orthodox you are. In such cases you would need a marriage Counselor that understands all these things, who is impartial and does not promote the welfare of one of you over the welfare of the other.

If you are modern, progressive and flexible then you should not seek the help of a rigid outmoded counselor. You are both better off without that. To my thinking a married marriage Counselor with a marriageable personality is better than a bachelor-personality marriage Counselor.

Physicians and Psychiatrists could offer an excellent marriage Counseling, especially when there are medical problems involved. Make sure you do not end up in a marriage quack's office, who creates eternal marriage problems for you to make a living.

Your compatibility tests should not lead to incompatibles operating in rings, contrary to your aims and interests to have a sound family life.

DIAGRAM illustrates the type of people that could help you; who could also be a terrible menace, if they are of an incompatible background, and acting without your consent.

Illustration 27

Diagram illustrates the type of people that could help you and who
could also be a terrible nuisance if things of an incompatible
background and acting without your consent.

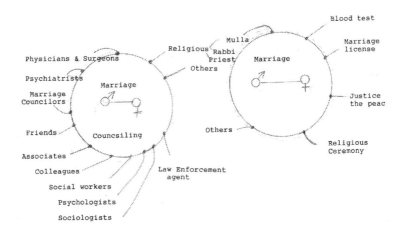

The Jury–

When a nonsectarian non-racial American is in trouble—non-marital, marital or post-marital, etc.—who would you disqualify as a Jurist:

Those who lack basic knowledge and do not quite believe in the Constitution of the USA?

Certain Categories of people whose knowledge of the USA Laws disqualify them from judging the Plaintiff and/or the Defendant?

Those who are too emotional to percept the truth?

Those having feelings of superiority over the Plaintiff and/or Defendant?

Mental recipes with concealed instincts for malice, jealousy, grudge, and injuries for others of different mental recipes?

Clergy; Religious Quacks?

Women? Homosexuals?

Industry people of Certain Categories?

Certain Categories of Doctors, Nurses and Pharmaceutical Personnel?

Reactions to The Following–

Do you think a man or woman who intentionally marries an incompatible mate is worthy to be—

A judge?	An Executive?	A Biochemist?
A Jurist?	A Movie star?	A policeman?
A Doctor?	An Engineer?	An Officer?
A Professor?	A Nurse?	A Sheriff?
A Lawyer?	A Publisher?	A cleaner?
An investigator?	A Business man?	An Industrialist?
A Marriage Counselor?	A Janitor?	A Bar tender?
A Clergy?	A Rabbi?	A moslem Mulla?
A Dentist?	A Dancing Instructor?	A Baker?
A Chiropractor?	An Accountant?	A Secretary?
A Laboratory Technologist?	A Manager?	A Pilate?
A typist?	A Librarian?	An Astronaut?
Other professions.		

Post "Marriage Dissolution" Period–

After your marriage is legally dissolved, you lose your Wife-Husband relations; you are no longer related any more than before you ever knew of each other.

The terms X-wife or X-husband indicate previous marriage which is finally dissociated and do not signify any present or future relations. The X- simply means nothing to your single unmarried or future marital status to other women.

Ethically and socially it is considered poor manners to keep wearing your wedding rings; also it is poor manners for the woman to keep her X-husband's name after final marriage dissolution.

By losing your wedding rings you might acquire an X-ring, especially if they are not satisfied with the Court's decisions.

When the X-ring is a secret society ring, then pestering you and persecuting you will have many forms and facets. It will not be a

Court action the way you had your marriage dissolved. This is called "setting things in the Underground because ....'

If your X-mate is not a secret society mate then nothing nuisance happens to you. In such cases the sincere partner will be facing the wall no matter what he does to correct the situation or convert the incompatible situation to a compatible one. Of course with one incompatible partner to begin with it is impossible to do so.

Lack of sexual harmony or marriage not based on true love and sex is a serious problem and it is best to always avoid it.

How can you and your mate be injured through a false or true? A Compatibility problem. For example if you are a doctor of a certain specialty, how can your patients be deviated away from you in the name of an allegation?

You will be put into an "off base" status. The form looks like this, before filling the blanks:

> You have to..............
> You will have troubles with your..........
> You have.........you have to come.......
> You use to be.............
> You have not............
> You have to...........
> You do not...........

Chapter

28

What is an X-Ring?

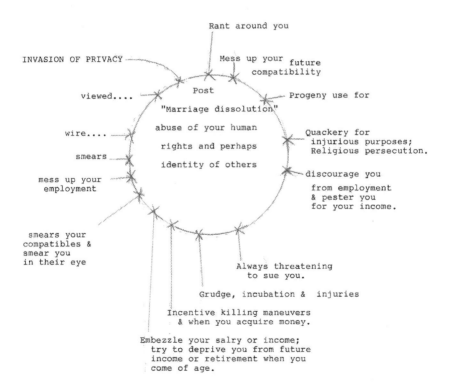

Illustration 28

WHAT IS AN X-RING ?

It is a legalized illegal or an illegal "mental recipe" or activity, operating in your post"marriage dissolution" time.

Rant around you

INVASION OF PRIVACY

Mess up your future compatibility

viewed....

Post "Marriage dissolution" abuse of your human rights and perhaps identity of others

Progeny use for

wire....

smears

Quackery for injurious purposes; Religious persecution.

mess up your employment

discourage you from employment & pester you for your income.

smears your compatibles & smear you in their eye

Always threatening to sue you.

Grudge, incubation & injuries

Incentive killing maneuvers & when you acquire money.

Embezzle your salry or income; try to deprive you from future income or retirement when you come of age.

IF YOU ARE ONE OF THOSE UNFORTUNATE WITH A CRUDE HOLDING "X" 'S YOU WOULD NEED TO

BE ALERT WITH ETERNAL VIGIL. THAT BY ITSELF
WOULD DISCOURAGE MANY COMPATIBLES. IT
WOULD BRIGHTEN YOUR LIFE. THE SADDEST THING
IS WHEN THE "X" 'S DO NOT REALIZE THAT HE/SHE IS
INCOMPATIBLE.

Illustration 29

WHAT IS AN X-RING? (Continued)

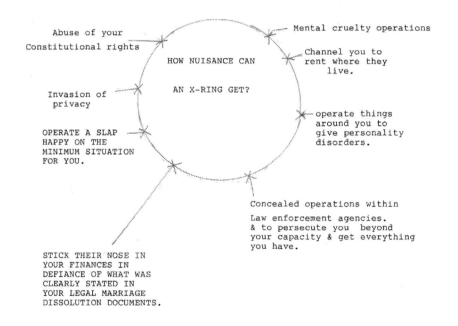

Abuse of your
Constitutional rights

Mental cruelty operations

HOW NUISANCE CAN

Channel you to
rent where they
live.

AN X-RING GET?

Invasion of
privacy

operate things
around you to
give personality
disorders.

OPERATE A SLAP
HAPPY ON THE
MINIMUM SITUATION
FOR YOU.

Concealed operations within

Law enforcement agencies.
& to persecute you beyond
your capacity & get everything
you have.

STICK THEIR NOSE IN
YOUR FINANCES IN
DEFIANCE OF WHAT WAS
CLEARLY STATED IN
YOUR LEGAL MARRIAGE
DISSOLUTION DOCUMENTS.

Illustration 30

WHAT IS AN X-RING (Continued)

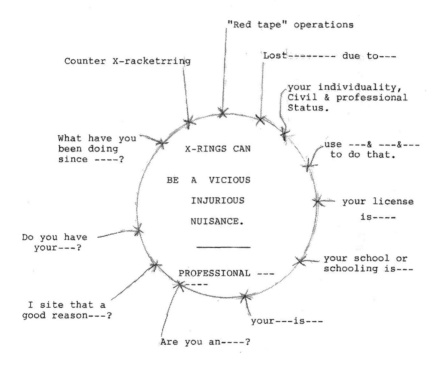

"Red tape" operations

Counter X-racketrring

Lost-------- due to---

your individuality,
Civil & professional
Status.

What have you
been doing
since ----?

X-RINGS CAN

BE A VICIOUS

INJURIOUS

NUISANCE.

use ---& ---&---
to do that.

your license
is----

Do you have
your---?

your school or
schooling is---

PROFESSIONAL ---

I site that a
good reason---?

your---is---

Are you an----?

Printed in the United States
By Bookmasters